Restoring My Soul

Dr Florence Hill St. Rose

ISBN 979-8-88751-336-2 (paperback)
ISBN 979-8-88832-991-7 (hardcover)
ISBN 979-8-88751-337-9 (digital)

Christian Faith Publishing
832 Park Avenue
Meadville, PA 16335
www.christianfaithpublishing.com

Printed in the United States of America

Introduction

I would like to dedicate this book to all the women out there in the world who have been victims of abuse and have been in strange turmoil in their lives. I want you to know that there is a way out. You have to put in the hard work to come out of your difficult emotional stress. If you are being told that you are nothing, that you cannot comprehend the fact while you are under their control, that you are a simple-minded woman, please know that Jesus sits on the throne 24-7, and he sees all and knows all about your troubles. With just a little initiative on your part, you can get up and rise to excellence. In your life, you are somebody.

Rise up my sister.

Rise up in your troubles.

Rise up and make yourself know that you are a person with feelings and that you matter to God.

Rise up and take your place among the strong black women.

Rise up and say to yourself, "I am worth more than this sorrow."

Rise up and say to this world, "I will get up and make something of myself instead of being someone's slave."

Rise up and say, "I am not someone's plaything. I am a human being just like they are, and I love myself enough to say that I am due respect."

This can be done in your life. It is going to take hard work and dedication, but you can do it. I am writing this book because I have lived all the horrors that you are living now. It is not for you to become self-centered or impossible to deal with. It is for you to become a humble human being and for you to give your life to

Christ, and he will do the rest. Thank you very much for buying this book. I hope that your dreams may be fulfilled and that you will go on and be a success in life.

—Dr. Florence St. Rose

I t was a very hot day when I was born. The woman who had my me
and twin did not want us. I could feel this even when we were not
born yet. I knew in my heart that something was wrong because
I never fitted in with the other children. They always whispered and
laughed when we were around. People were nice but far away in their
actions. They did their best, but there was always something missing
in my life. As I grew, there were many happy events, like going to
church with my adopted mother. This was my number one priority.

We would worship the Lord and pray to him every Sunday.
There was singing, and everyone would have a joyful time in the
Lord. People were talking. There was a lot of food. Anything you
could think of was on that table: chicken, greens, corn, sweet potatoes, white potatoes, cornbread, rolls, etc. I went to the table four
times to fill my plate. You see, I had a tank for a stomach. That
would never end. I would watch all the people around me. When
they shouted and praised the Lord, it would move me quickly to get
me out of the way. They were good people who helped other people
at all times.

At five years old, I was playing in the yard. My mother wanted
to visit a friend who was down the street. Little did I know that there
was a child molester in the alley. Then he told me, "Come here," and
I did not fear him because he was a friend of the family. He abused
me, and when he saw my mom, he told me to ride my bike up the
hill as fast as I could. I did not tell my mom because I was ashamed.
My self-worth was gone, and my confidence was gone. In those days,
the grown-ups were believed, and the children were dismissed.

I know this has probably happened to most of you as you are reading this book. I want you to know that you can overcome the devil with the blood of the Lamb and the word of your testimony. Love not your soul unto death but to life. Although you have been abused, that does not mean you have to go down a destructive path. It is up to you to succeed in your life because your life is valuable to God.

Here are things that affect you when you have been abused. You do not feel good about yourself. People don't look at you the same way they used to. Everything is black in your world, and you long for freedom from your bondage of pain. In the head of a five-year-old, he or she is asking themselves, "Why?"

I did not want to be around men. I would shy away from people when I was small. My time was spent in the house, not wanting to go anywhere except with my mother. No one knew my secret, and no one knew my shame.

In the ninth grade, someone tried to rape me, but he did not succeed. When you are a homebody, men tend to think that you are easy because you are inexperienced in the world, and they know it.

My most difficult time in life was making it through high school. I had a learning disability and still do. Most people have called me dumb. I did not understand most of the books they wrote. Studying was very hard for me because of my learning disability. I had to work harder than other students. Hanging out was popular, and going to clubs after church was a knockout. Yes, my friend, if you were with the in crowd and you had a boyfriend and were fulfilling all his desires, everything was like apple pie. Girlfriend, you were not respected. You were just a whore to him and everyone else, and all his friends knew it because he told them. I'm going to tell you how it is!

The Bible said in 1 Corinthians 5 that having sex without marriage is an abomination to God. We have to look beyond that. We have to place value on ourselves. We were not made to be doormats; we were made to be a helpmate to all men and marry them, not to be a slut to them. When a woman and a man stand before God and wait before marriage, this is acceptable to God, and he will bless the union. This is faithful on both ends because you respected his wishes and commandments.

Everybody seems to think what you were doing was just fine, but you see, it was not to God. How much do you love yourself and respect yourself and say "I will not shame myself and my family"? He is not going to marry you! He will tell you that it did not work out, and he will move on to the next one. Stay in school and keep your legs closed! Education is the key to your success. What you really need is Jesus Christ in your life.

I went to Sunday school as a teacher with my mother's hat turned to the side, thinking I was popular and pretending to be saved. I was just a good actor, that's all. I sang in the chorus, but my soul was lost to the Lord because I was not sincere. Come on, you know we all did that because all we were thinking about was that hole in the wall, which was the club. This book gave me a change of heart about a lot of things in my life and yours also because you are not all that either.

Parents, listen to me very carefully. Know what your teenagers are doing and thinking—day and night, night and day. Take the time to listen to them when they want to talk to you. You must have a mother-and-daughter dinner night out, and one with your sons also. If you don't, you will have babies on both ends before you know it—just because you did not take the time to talk to them. The youth have a voice, and they want to be heard! Please listen to them. Have a session around the table at night and find out how their day was— not just one but every day. Try to stay on top of their activities every day. Put your children in sports, music, or other things that they might like. They can't get there by themselves. Where are you when they are at home trying to raise themselves? You cannot raise them from the bars. You have a commitment to them. They did not ask to be here. You had sex and had them. Clean up your life and clean up you corrupt spirit before it is too late. Be a part of their lives, and they will be a part of yours also.

> Correct thy son, and he shall give thee rest; yea,
> he shall give delight unto thy soul. (Proverbs
> 29:17)

Inside, there is a sense of desperation and despair in my heart. Sometimes, I would ask God, "What am I doing here?"

You see, when you have no substance in your life, going on day-to-day begins to be a drag. I was never at ease anywhere I went. There had to be something more to life. Trying to figure it out was heartbreaking to me. It is almost like pushing a rope off a hill and getting nowhere. Also, it feels like walking a tightrope with no safety net below.

> He restores my soul, he leadeth me in the path of righteousness, for his name's sake, ye do I walk though the valley of the shadow of death, I will fear no evil. For though rod, the staff, they comfort me. (Psalm 23:3–4)

After high school, the army recruited me. To me, it was a dream come true, or so I thought, but they left out the nine weeks of hell you have to go through to succeed. Believe me. I know what I am talking about. While you were riding the bus, everything was wonderful. As soon as you got off, yelling and screaming began when another person in uniform came on the bus. I asked myself if I was in my right mind when I signed up to go into the service. I could not hear myself think when all that spit was flying on my face as I dragged my suitcase up the stairs. I asked God, "Why me?" I said to myself that I was crazy to sign up.

Things were rough for a while. Every day, there was something different. Woah, woah, woah, you could hear the drill sergeants before they came into the room. When I passed all my courses, I fell out. Thank you, Jesus. I have made it.

I asked my sergeants, "Do you have the right person?"

The mess hall was really fun! Drop your fork and take a bow, because everyone would clap when that happens. Can you imagine black coarse hair done with a Tony? Well! All my friends cornered me and gave me one. It turned out very well. Well, I was happy. In class, you had to keep one eye open for class and one eye closed for sleep. Little did I know that more sin was at my door.

The Lord is my light and my salvation; whom
shall I fear? The Lord is the strength of my life; of
whom shall I be afraid?

Time and time again, you have said to yourself, "I am not going
to let this happen again," and it has. Girlfriend, you might as well be
in quicksand. Jesus is the only answer to your problems. Men in your
life will test you. They are going to see if you will do what they want
you to do. Believe me, a fool is born every minute.

You began to become a puppet on a string, and he was the one
pulling it. Soon, you found yourself doing everything in the house as
you should as a faithful wife and not a faithful girlfriend.

You see, a girlfriend will not be faithful. She will be faithful only
when the money flows. Sometimes, you will find yourself paying all
the bills because you are the only one working and he is not! Are you
feeling me, sister? I hope you are. It is not that we, as black women,
don't have sense; we just love with everything we have, and sometimes we don't get that in return.

In some cases, men take advantage of a woman in love. Did you
know that Jesus has a plan for your life? Just ask him what it is, and
he will tell you. Okay, we all make wrong decisions in our lives, so
rise up, repent, ask God to help you, and try again with the common
sense of what you have learned from the wrong decisions of the past.
Try it again with strength and really get a sense of security. Just do
hard work on your part. It can be done. If I can see a ninety-year-old
couple in school.

Tell me, girlfriend, what is wrong with you! Don't get lazy and
complain. Get serious and go get your dreams from your past, put
them in your future, and make them come true. You cannot give up
now, and you should stop saying you cannot do it because the devil
will make it come true. You don't want to fail. You want to succeed
in this lifetime. Rise up and claim your rights as an important human
being who is not known as a roll in the hay—which means, in Jesus's
eyes, you have been labeled as a whore. Come to him, confess your
sins, and let him direct your life. Get in church and learn all about

his commandments and laws. No one said it was going to be easy, but God will lighten your load.

Get yourself together and say, "I am somebody. I am somebody, and I am sound and free from bondage. Free at last. Free at last. Thank you, God Almighty, I am free at last!"

The Cat to the Mouse

"Well, well, well," said the cat to the mouse. "Come into my home. I will not eat you."

But we all know that it is a lie. Get this, girlfriend. He buys you beautiful clothes, wines and dines you, and you end up saying to yourself that he is the one. Then you are in lust, and you have drunk too much. You don't even know what day it is. I know you want to say that it is not you, but it is. He is the most handsome man in your life, and naturally, you want to do anything in your power to keep him. So you tell your friends that you can make it without them.

You wonder what happened to his attitude, and he says over and over again the following things:

> I will be there for you.
> Look at what I did for you.
> Look at all the nice clothes and jewelry that you
>   have.
> I have brought you a big house, and you have
>   money to spend.
> You don't need to go out, just stay with me.
> I am your sugar daddy, and you can rely on me,
>   sugar lips.

But in time, you will learn that they were just big lies from the pits of hell. Tell me, girlfriend, did an alarm go off in your head? Get the hell out while you can, but you stay because you have fallen in love with the jerk. Do you feel me, sister? Oh, no. Don't tell me you were deceived. What do you do now? There are two things you can do. You can pack up your bags and leave and escape the abuse and the hardship, or you can stay and go through it, and as sure as I am writing this book, you will become a slave to him.

I had accomplished my dream, but little did I know that it would turn out to be a nightmare in the flesh. Little by little, he would tell me, "You don't know anything. You're a dumb country ass, and you're a dumb bitch! I need you like I need a hole in my head."

He was programming me for servanthood. Get it, girlfriend. Read between the lines, slave. Everything will begin to take a toll on you. Your self-esteem will begin to fade in time. You will become a walking and talking zombie.

You did not think that he would say those things to you. Your stomach is tied up in knots, and your head feels like it is going to explode. Your emotions are running high. Tell me, girlfriend, have I hit a spot in your lonely life? Because you see, after dinner, he was gone, and you were left alone with the children. What is your point of view when the same thing happens every night? You have become old to him, and the thrill is gone!

Do you know which way you are going, girlfriend, or are you drowning in your own self-pity? Have you ever surfaced for air? Let me tell you! He has not gone out to be with the good old boys. If others have sense, they are home with their family. Remember, I said there were very few of them. The rest are hunting for fresh meat— not you, but someone else. He is not going to feel sorry for you.

You see, you did this to yourself by not fulfilling your dreams and staying your butt in school. You just had to see what was in the clubs, and now you know! Your life is filled with pain and suffering to your despair, but there is a solution to your problem. Rise up and take control of your life. Read the signs. You are not walking beside him. You are walking behind him as his personal slave. You have to depend on him for money and a house to live in and food for your children.

When did you surrender your self-worth to him? He does not love you. He is just using you until he gets his fill, and after that, he is gone. What will you do? Where did it all go wrong in your and his life? He does not introduce you to his friends because he is ashamed of you because you are not educated, and your English is broken. That is the truth. Your body is broken down, and you don't look like you used to have his babies, and they are the only ones who get a names.

1. First came a slap, and then, in front of the children, he called you a bitch.
2. He picked out old ladies' clothes for you.
3. The mental and physical abuse goes on, and you don't know what to do.
4. You get beat down every other day.

He promises that he will not hit you again, but we all know that it is a lie. By now, you are entering a state of hopelessness and believing that Jesus can't forgive you, but don't believe the lie. The sex became like pushing a rope up a hill with no substance or feeling in your heart. Those are the duties of a wife, but the thrill is gone! What shall we do? Sex with him was like paint drying on the wall and chipping off because it was cheap paint and not the real thing. Only a well-thought-out plan. You see, after he comes home, he does not have anything left. What used to be an hour turned into a minute. You know the drill, girlfriend! While he should have been home with you, he was rolling in the hay with someone else!

1. He separated you from your family.
2. No telephone calls or communication.
3. He caused conflict between both families by turning them against each other.
4. He gathered all the dirt from your background by having you talk about yourself, only to rub it in later by telling you, "You were out there before I met you!"
5. You wanted to be honest with him, so you told him every-thing. But, girlfriend, you have just condemned yourself to a lifetime of hell.

6. He has all the information because, naturally, you do not want any secrets in your relationship. You tried to be honest.
7. When the honeymoon period is over, you knew it because he called you a bitch and a hoe.
8. You are the one who armed him with all the confessions about yourself when it was supposed to be between you and Jesus, because you are not that same person anymore.
9. You say to yourself, "Where did the love go?"
10. Men talk more than women. They know who will and know who will not. Girlfriend, beware! Sometimes, a smile can be fangs instead of teeth!
11. Welcome to your worst nightmare, girlfriends!

Let us be perfectly frank, we all have hang-ups. Also, if you do not know Jesus before you get involved, it would be a good idea to seek him out first. We bring baggage with us to the relationship. The last boyfriend you had or the last husband you had did not understand you in your hour of need. Soul ties are real when someone goes outside of the relationship, marriage or not. Well, let me tell you the ropes, girlfriend!

1. They stay with a girlfriend for only three months.
2. Then they will shop around for another partner besides you.
3. You are left brokenhearted, and you wonder what happened to the relationship.
4. You were too young to get involved with an older man.
5. You did not have any business engaging in sexual relations with him.
6. My slogan is "No sex education is the key!" You must love and respect yourself first.
7. Respect yourself and keep God's temple clean—that means your body!
8. Why would you be so quick to lose all you have just to satisfy someone's hormones running wild in his body?

9. You will just become another conquest in his life, and right about now, your stuff is old!

There are diseases that eat up medicine for breakfast, lunch, and dinner. Why would you become someone's whore and have people talk about you that way? They will say ugly things about you. Would you just be a host for a disease that cannot be destroyed—without knowing Jesus because hell is real. Listen, girlfriend, you are not popular; you are easy. Read it and weep!

Example 1

You are out with your boyfriend, and he takes you to a bar, and all his friends are there. They seem to surround you and admire you. They look at you up and down like a popsicle. You look beautiful, and you can't get over yourself from all the attention, but in the back of their minds, they are waiting for their turn because you are not a decent girl. You are a hoe, and they want you to be one. Your so-called boyfriend has told them all about how easy you were to conquer, and they do not respect you at all. The truth is they wish they could get you drunk, take you home themselves, and disappear in the morning. I'm going to tell you the truth. You are not marriage material, and they are not going to marry you after everyone has had you! Because you never said no to them or took the time to say no to yourself. Even your boyfriend has labeled you also. After three months, he is gone, and all your dreams with him! This brings me to the conclusion in our lives that we are a pushover, and we don't love ourselves enough to say no.

1. You don't love yourself enough to say, "No, I am worth more than this."
2. You don't love yourself enough to say that if to say to yourself. If he does not put a ring on it, he does not deserve you at all!
3. Put a value on yourself. I ask you, "What are you worth?"

If you don't want a college education, there are things you can do:

1. On-the-job training at the college. It pays between thirty-five to fifty thousand a year working outdoors.
2. You can get a four-year degree at a community college.
3. They will pay your mother to keep the babies.
4. You can get food stamps.
5. You can get transportation to and from school.
6. If you don't want a four-year degree, get a two-year degree.
7. If your learning is off, take pre-courses until you get it.
8. If you don't have anyone to take care of the babies, take them out to the college and put them in childcare also. They will pay for the childcare.

Example 2
The Wedding Night

You have just come from the perfect wedding of your dreams, and everything is perfect in your eyes. All of a sudden, his friends came over and wanted to take him out for drinks. As he began to talk, he did not know that, as a big dummy, he was giving his so-called friends ammunition to blackmail his wife. He got up in the morning, and he was so full of life, but his friends were planning to come to his house. They pretended that he was home, but they knew the unsuspecting fool had left for work. They were planning to have sex with his wife because they wanted the same thing that he had the night before. Before his tires could hit the curb, here came his so-called friends, and they knew she was not dressed yet. She opened the door because she was young and inexperienced, and they began to pass her and rub up against her. She did not know what to do.

If you were a young newlywed, never, never, never open the door to his socalled friends because you would become a whore and a slave. The intentions were good, but the moral was not! They took advantage of her and seduced her—all of them. And they kept blackmailing her until she packed her bags and left the house. He could understand why his wife was gone. She could not tell him the truth because she was trapped in her mind and body. He himself began to call her a bitch and complain to his so-called buddies, but they would all gather around and tell him that she was not any good for him. Fool! They would all agree among themselves. He had no business telling anyone about his business. That night was supposed to be a sacred night between his bride, God, and himself. They had ruined his life, and he did not know the truth. The sacred vow that was made on that night has been dissolved forever.

When it comes to your friends, they are not your friends when they are plotting against you. You have spoiled your own marriage by running your mouth when you should have kept your mouth shut. Now your so-called friends call you a fool, and they are laughing at you and calling you the biggest fool in the world. Learn from your mistakes! PS: Do you think they are going to tell you about their sex life? Think about it, and think about it really hard!

Example 3
Easy Conquest

You were at the bar drinking, and you knew you should not be there. You should have been at home with your kids, but you were at the bar. He was looking at you, but what was he thinking? He was thinking that you didn't have too much between your ears and would be an easy conquest. Your heart was beating so fast that you could not contain yourself.

You're mine, you said to yourself! *He is the one.*

He was saying to himself, *How can I get this fool into bed?*

In your mind, you were thinking about marriage and a little white house with children and in-laws, but his thoughts were different. He wanted to break you down so that he could have his own way with you. You took the chance with this guy because you wanted to please him. You gave up everything. Your self-respect and your self-worth were gone. To him, you were just an easy piece that he has on the side for fun. You were that fool! He took off his marriage band

and fooled you into taking part in sexual intercourse with him, or as they called it, *a tumble in the hay*!

He told you he had to go, and you were left alone to cry and see what a fool you had been. When you woke up, you would find money by the bed. You thought you were going to see him again, but to him, you were just a cheap whore. Your dreams were shattered. You had been kicked to the curb like feces, and your self-esteem was gone. You don't have to give your love to anyone or get approval from anyone. Respect yourself, and others will respect you! Be free from fornication and other sins by going to Jesus.

Respect yourself, and say to God, "Help me. I have had enough! Things that happen in the family, keep them in the family."

Example 4
Hot Pants

You think that you are so hot that people cannot do without you. You wear the right clothes, and you have a lot of money to spend. You buy everyone around you drinks, and you don't have enough money to pay your bills at the end of the month. You want to impress men so much that you forget about Jesus Christ, your Savior.

Mom has cut you off. Dad has cut you off. And you don't have anywhere to turn to. You have a nickname! The drunks assumed a lot, and your conscience is almost gone. Like we say, girlfriend, you think that you know what's happening? But when it comes down to it, you are, in the eyes of the Lord, just a low-down dirty hoe. You don't know who he is, where he came from, or when he left. You just have to have a man! There have been so many in your life. You cannot count them on your fingers.

We should cry out to Jesus, confess our sins, get our past, present, and future clean, and start all over again. You see, the devil said that God will not forgive you, but Jesus will, and his arms are ready and wide open to receive you. Oh, happy day! Pay your 10 percent in church. If you have fifty cents and you pay 25 percent, Jesus will honor it. Take a chance on him, and he will take a chance on you. He will know that you are doing your best, and he will bless you for it.

Just give him a chance! He is love, and you will be his child. He will take care of you. Just believe in him! Your life will begin to change, and wonderful things will happen in your life because he chases those that he loves. Jesus will clean you up, and you will become a new person. Your name will be written in the Book of Life, which sits by his throne! The angels will rejoice. One more soul for the kingdom of God.

Example 5
Baby Boy Expose

It is Christmas time, and everyone in the family is merry and thankful to God. The children are wide-eyed, and they're being especially good and quiet because they know that the big day will soon be tomorrow. You have invited your so-called best friend over to the Christmas party, and naturally, everyone is excited because they have made it to the next year. You are not aware that the baby boy you are playing with is your husband. He makes a stop at a belt store and picks up a gift. He buys two gifts instead of one. You notice it on the sales slip. Then you question him about it, and he says to you, "Look at it again. You made a mistake." But you know that he did not.

You wonder who was the other for. You also notice that your best friend is wearing the same scent that you are wearing. You began to freak out because you know his secret. Okay, you put your children to bed, and you close the doors to their room. You confront your husband, and naturally, the goofball lies, but you continue to pound him until he confesses to the affair.

Your heart is broken, but there are children involved. So you swallow your pride and suck it in, and you go on because the babies are more important than he is. Surprise! You have found out about more children. And you say to yourself, *They are innocent, but the parents are not.*

You cry yourself to sleep at night, and you turn your back to him. He has not only failed you but himself as well. With Jesus at my side, I know that all things are possible. More women think that they are not worth anything because they have been listening to that unnecessary abuse from men, telling them that they are not worth anything, but that is a lie from the pits of hell.

Rise up my sister and remember the following:

1. Take control of your life.
2. Keep your legs shut and keep your eyes on the prize, which is the Lord Jesus Christ.
3. You do not need a man to make you happy.
4. You don't need to waste your life and lose your self-respect to keep a man.
5. Say to yourself, "I love myself."
6. We are all born imperfect, but so what? God will help me in my dilemma.
7. Maybelline and CoverGirl were my best friend.
8. The black eyes and black marks on my forehead were from being beaten by extension and electric cords.
9. My mind was completely gone.
10. Most times, I was in a very dark place.
11. I was lost in my mind, and my soul and body were lost to the world.
12. I could not function as a human being.
13. He knew what he was doing to me.
14. He did not want a wife; he wanted a 24-7 slave.
15. God was on my side, and he delivered me.
16. Little by little, he emptied out my nasty body that was full of soul ties from women and men infested with demons.
17. All this happened because I did not know who he was and what he was.

But one day, I saw the light in my bedroom. I was reading the Bible, and my whole room lit up. Just as if I was at a carnival, and in each window, there was a light. You see, girlfriend, I had been asking God to deliver me for a long time. He took his own time about it because, on my wedding day, he was screaming in my ear, "Do not marry that demon or man."

Out of my disobedience, I married him, and all hell broke loose in my life. And out of my own disobedience, I suffered long, and so did my children. Even though I was married, my children were attacked by the enemy. They were attacked in life. When you have children out of wedlock, they can be attacked, not being under God's covering. Read it and weep! Girlfriend, I was a fool! Do not be one!

If you want to be a good wife, do the following:

1. Put a ring on it and wait for sex!
2. Get counsel from a real preacher, not from the ones who don't do right themselves!
3. Wait out your wants and diswants about each other
4. Get in church and pay your 10 percent to God—both of you.
5. Get a job, save your money, and work toward a future!
6. Learn from your minister to talk out your problems and not fight in sin and strife, holding out against each other.
7. Come together in love instead of hate.
8. Learn to love yourself first, and then learn to love your husband and others as well.
9. Ask Jesus to help you throughout your life and for both of you to respect each other's feelings!
10. Love your neighbor as you would love yourself. When someone comes to you talking about someone else, walk away and do not join in because, in the same way, if you talk about someone else with them, they will be saying not-so-good things about you too!

In the eyes of Jesus, I was a whore and not his child until he chose to clean me up. My life was in turmoil. I was betrayed by my feelings of love for my husband, but he had no love for me, only service. He beat me and terrorized me every chance he got, but the Lord Jesus Christ revived me and delivered me to freedom!

It is a funny thing when you think you are in love, and you give up everything that you have. But you have to ask yourself, "Is it love or just plain sex that he wants?"

Jesus taught me about self-respect and that he loves me and that he takes me just as I am. He changed my life for the better. As I matured, when older women would ask if I had a boyfriend, I would just say yes, but now I knew what they meant.

When I see young girls pregnant, it hurts me! There is no future, no honor, and no self-respect because you made a mistake in your life, but we can correct that! We have an unlimited amount of learning to do, just enough to get a nonmeaning job. Get yourself back in school! That is the only chance you have. Tell me, how is a baby girl or boy going to teach a baby anything when they don't know anything themselves? Broken English and rapping to a beat are not going to make it for them.

The world has gone to hell in a handbasket, and we're along with it. We, as parents, should rise up and tell our girls to say no! I am worth more than that. If they have a baby or have an abortion, that will affect them, also.

Mothers, we have to do better. Fathers, we must teach our sons to respect women and not abuse them. Spend time with them and let them know that a good wife is worth waiting for. Look at them and ask yourself how you were brought up! And would you like someone to treat you or your family like that?

Men, we must teach him or her to be a respectable man or woman, first to God and then to man, because when a man finds a good wife, he finds a good thing. The same thing goes for a good husband.

If the storms come, you will know how to oversee them in Christ Jesus. There will be good days and bad days, but remember, you will have God on your side. Remember what brought you together, and then think about the good times you had together and weather out the storms.

God is love, and he loves us unconditionally. Why can't we do the same for each other? Remember to keep your faith because faith will bring you through to a good and better life in your future.

Thank you.

—Dr. Florence St. Rose

About the Author

Good afternoon, my family and friends.

My name is Florence St. Rose.

I had a pretty fair childhood, and I did well in most of my classes. My message to you is to not let people get you down; don't let them get into your head. I have a disability, you know, understanding sometimes. But I didn't let that stop me from completing the tests of life. There had been much abuse in my life and much mistreatment too. It has not been all joy.

Jesus said, "If the Son shall set you free, you shall be free indeed." This means you are not only free in your mind but in your soul and body as well.

During my tests, trials, and tribulations, I learned to have patience and keep talking to the Lord and reading my Bible. Through this time of turmoil, God healed me, forgave me for my sins, and set me free.

I now have a BA, a master's, and a PhD in ministry. I am an ordained elder in the church of the New Beginning Christian Center in Jacksonville. There is no such thing as I can't because we can do the hard work and complete God's will. That's right. It is very hard work, but it can be done. We came from a poor family, and my father left when we were small, but that did not stop me. I was intended to finish the work, and with God's help, I did.